"No Crying
He Makes ..."

by Miriam S. Lind

D1292203

HERALD PRESS

SCOTTDALE, PENNSYLVANIA

Contents

A Litany of Thanks

Thanks to Ruth

Who, out of all who knew our need, alone came forward and said, "I'll be a mother to the child. Now run along and have a good year." More thanks, that she and her family saw not a burden but an opportunity; not a duty but a joy. (And she brought violets from the woods for my Memory Garden. . . .)

Thanks to Abba

Who looks up from his study of The Book just often enough to reinforce this woman with his love; to excite his sons with his wisdom; to make his daughter's countenance shine at his tenderness; and to gladden the heart of BuBu with a walk to the playground via the Soda Shop.

Thanks to Sarah

Who takes without complaint — well, usually — much putting-upon; who shares the mothering of BuBu at least by half; who reads, sings, walks, talks with him; who makes beanbags and under-the-table houses and all manner of Curious Original Games, and plays them with him; who disciplines, comforts, feeds, bathes, and on occasion puts to bed the child deserted by this woman; who does it all with a light touch with no asking for shekels for the purse or jewels for a crown.

Thanks to the Brothers: To Dan

Whose years with BuBu were few, but who contributed more the child's well-being than he realizes — in the painting of walls and cupboards; in spreading the propaganda for an automatic dishwasher once-upon-a-Mother's-Day; and in giving to us Anne, and through Anne, small Dirk. (Thanks to Anne who in addition to other evidences of love, came early on Dinner-Evenings in order to enjoy BuBu.)

Thanks to Jonathan

Who daily infuses the family with life; who speaks as he thinks, who asks questions, tells us off, laughs at himself, mispronounces words, and limbers us all, so preventing us from taking ourselves and our tasks too seriously.

Thanks to Timothy

Who sees life whole — what is apparent and what is hidden — and lives according to this deepset vision; who speaks sparingly with his mouth and lavishly with the gifts of his hands — a poem, a new-tiled floor, a blue-walled kitchen. . . .

Thanks to Matthew

Who alone of all the family males is able to put the child to bed with firmness enough to keep him there and with gentleness enough to keep him happy; who cares about BuBu, about the family, about his friends, about all lonely and hurt and frightened Ones. Praise be for his deep angers and his fierce loyalties.

Thanks to James

Who oversees BuBu's leg exercises; who works cunningly with wood and lathe and with rod and reel; who fixes chairs, wagons, trikes, faucets; who prepares gourmet food for the family in the absence of this woman, and leaves the kitchen floor sticky to walk upon.

Thanks to Mary

The friend who loves at all times; who never pretends to be Nice when she feels Otherwise; who in the long babyhood of BuBu came to our door asked or unasked and made bearable the isolation of this woman by discussing with her all manner of exciting subjects such as Hymnals, Death, Excellence, Toothpicks, Grace, Students, Africa, Israel, and Isometric Exercises.

Thanks to Liz

Always there in the background inspiring, praising, thanking (and over-thanking), believing, and in general perpetuating our mother's kind of caring. Praise be for that one whose life-direction is indicated in her most automatic utterance: "Let me help."

Thanks to Aux Chandelles

Which daily leads the child further *Into the Light,*

stretching his mind, quickening his senses, enhancing his social graces, habilitating his speech, and — Praise be! — perfecting his toilet training. To its administrators, its teachers, its staff, and especially to the mothers of the Coffee Hour, this small book is dedicated.

m.s.l.

Prologue

Before his birth his unmarried mother arranged for her baby's adoption. But there were *two* babies born prematurely, and one did not survive. In spite of prematurity, RH incompatibility, and a severe respiratory infection resulting in a breathing-lapse, the other child clung to life. When brain damage was suspected, however, the proposed adoption evaporated.

Our family's application for a foster child was in the files of the Public Welfare Office. Would we be interested in taking this boy for a period of, say, five or six months until a "permanent solution" could be found? A poll of the family brought an immediate, unanimous "Yes." And so, when he graduated from tube to bottle at the age of two and one-half months, he came to us.

Like several of his new brothers he came to us in the middle of the night, weighing what our own newborns had weighed — a bit over nine pounds. Unlike them, he was already a veteran sufferer. In the few weeks since his birth he had been given more medical attention than our entire family had accumulated in its collective lifetime. Lifting the corner of the blanket, we saw a pale mound of flesh, barely responding to pressure, movement, or sound. But life was there, persistent life. And no matter how that life had come to us, no matter what its condition, our household again knew joy at the "birth" of another family member.

Scarcely were the Social Workers out the door when the Family came leaping and tumbling down the stairs: big bare boys in their briefs, littler boys in rumpled pajamas, and She, all brown eyes and long nightgown. The eight of us must have looked like the creche figures of Joseph and Mary, shepherds and wise men, as we gathered around the bassinet that first night, wondering what our brand of caring could do for one small child.

This brief account isn't meant to be a story or case-history of that child. It is not an objective report of his growth or of our part in aiding that growth. It is meant to be a sampling of *feelings* stirred up by personal involvement. Admittedly these feelings are not particularly disciplined, and the mood may seem erratic and ambivalent. If so, a little piece of honesty has been communicated, for on this subject (as well as some others) my feelings are erratic and ambivalent.

The vehicles used to arrive at my destination are varied: narration, introspective probing, recollection, documentation, recrimination, hymn-singing — anything but "cool-headed logic." (Logic is an irrelevancy in our milieu.) If extraneous matter appears, I can only defend it by insisting that it is not foreign to the situations, but is an integral factor in the feelings arising within and around and in-reflection-upon my life with BuBu. Past-time and future-time have a way of superimposing themselves upon the present, and neither memory nor fantasy always waits to be invited. Without warning, the Now is pierced by the Then, and sometimes in the process bubbles burst. Or warmth suffuses, or cold contracts, or a kind of adrenalin revives the spirit. I have tried to include at least a sampling of these disruptions.

There is anger here, unreason, and sentiment-gone-to-seed as sentimentality. (Forgive us our defenses; we parents of special children tend to favor the latter sin in order to escape the clutches of the first two.) There's a painful listing of hurts and judgments here which an objective writer would temper. But I don't mean, even at the outset, to pass as either temperate or wise, for I am neither. I *mean* to blurt out my hostility and sing out my love. And if a few intermediate, domesticated emotions find their way into this account, they too should be permitted to give their testimony in court!

I want to open a window — one window — on the life of a child, a family, a community, and to chronicle some of their interaction and reaction. It's only *one* window, and what this one window reveals may not be all that helpful to people looking in. Many parents of retarded, physically handicapped, or foster children (BuBu possesses all three of these "impairments") have written more insightful, literary, and objective accounts of their children. Is this small book really necessary?

Not really, I suppose. Still, in revealing one particular scene and one way of viewing it and responding to it, I hope to articulate at least a bit of the tedium, joy, concern, fun, and heaviness of other parents of special children. Most of those parents — at least the ones I know — manage to practice more charity and restraint than I've indulged in here. Because they, unlike us, did not *choose* to have a special child, they have additional problems we've been spared. (And they may have been spared a few others which we inherited with our choice.) They may feel more vulnerable, less free to expose the raw edge of their emotional reactions. But you can be sure that their feelings, like mine, run the distance from resentment (which I prefer to call *hatred* or, at the least, *hostility*) through acceptance, to gratitude.

The road we take with a special child is a quieter road than the main highway — a road on which there is no drag-racing nor murderous striving to pass. It is the kind of road on which one must *walk*, and where one may do so with safety and pleasure. There's a bit of grass between the tracks and the roadsides are wilder, less cropped, and free of billboards and traffic instructions. Few people know how to enjoy walking here, after rushing about, executing their "busy schedules." But we've learned. And in walking such a road with such a child we have discovered new wonders of life and new powers of love.

"The cattle are lowing, the poor baby wakes,
The Little Lord Jesus, no crying He makes."

From Luther's **Cradle Hymn.**

1

"Yes ...
and
Always Yes"

The TV weather report promises 95 degrees for tomorrow — again. And with high humidity. Now at midnight a breath of cool air stirs in our warm room. But I can't sleep, and so I move out to the kitchen. Why can't I sleep? Is it coffee? Worry? Fatigue?

Not coffee, surely — only one cup at breakfast, one at lunch.

Maybe a bit of worry?

Maybe. . . . First Son, on his maiden-flight from home, is in the sophisticated colony of musicians at Aspen. Dear God, he's so young. . . .

We sit on the edge of the lower bunk and I am repeating on request the story of Small Jesus and the Wise Men. His sturdy little body is smelling of Ivory soap, his crew cut bristles pleasantly scratching the tender skin under my chin. Suddenly there's that incandescent blaze of hope in his eyes

15

as he looks up and whispers, "Did people think *I* was a king?" The shy ducking of the head, the quick, embarrassed reply, infinitely sad, barely audible — "No, people didn't think I was a king."

O little Son, why didn't you give me time to answer? To say, "Your daddy would hold you up — you just filled his two hands — and he'd cry out, MY PRINCE!" . . .

I lean against the upper bunk in the bedtime ritual of stories, kisses, prayers, talk. You've had a large day — your first day of school. "Mommy, what is a asp?"

"Use it in a sentence — "

"Well this boy on the bus said to me, *I'll kick your asp.*"

(Good upright little mother, now give your child a careful answer, one that will divide the sheep from the goats. . . . How did I say it? Did I call it a crude word for "bottom"? And what factors in these intervening twenty years have so modified my concept of "good" and "bad" words? . . .

Those bedtimes! Why do they come back tonight, in such a torrent of sweetness?

"Tell me about the time your mommy spanked you for sitting in the ditch." "Tell me about the Three Hebrew Children!" "Tell me about when Daddy got switched for crossing the road!"

I love you, God bless you, you are very special to me. . . .

"How am I special, Mommy?"

Well, for one thing, you are the only one who keeps cool when someone is hurt; you don't jump up and down and scream — you help the hurt person, you call us, you pick up the pieces. You are the only — Good night, I love you. . . . Yes, my mother always kissed me good night too, and if I'd been fighting with one of my sisters, she'd say, *Girls, don't let the sun go down on your wrath; now kiss each other and say, Forgive me.*

(It was a good rule, even though we often felt like spitting into those ears instead of whispering, "Forgive me." O My Mother, why didn't you stay long enough to be my children's grandmother?)

Dear God, he's so young. . . . Strange, it's at the table I miss him most, but he keeps popping into my consciousness tonight as this little blond kid I'm putting to bed. . . .

BOYS! QUIET!

"But Mom, we're just telling dreams to each other. . . ."

"And Satan said to God, why did you kill that wolf, and God said, I didn't kill him, he died hisself when he'd aten that rotten apple."

The brown-haired one sighs — I can hear the almost-sob from my room — "You tell good dreams, Danny."

"Yeah, but yours are excitinger. Now you."

The piping rise and fall of the younger voice now drifts in to me: "This little strong boy who wasn't strong . . . he dint have ANY strong in him so he prayed to God to give him some but God dint give him any strong. Then this little strong boy that wasn't strong he — he — he KILLED A MONSTER — " Now he's shivering in the dark, I know, and his great brown eyes are glistening with tears of excitement — "And after he killed that monster, some STRONG came into him. It really did. . . ."

Dear God! He's so young — so easily impressed. Will the values we assumed he had chosen for himself prove to have been merely ours after all?

Sometimes I think I shall have to learn to pray all over again — I who in years past glibly tried to teach others to believe in prayer. Enough, tonight, to repeat for the blond violist: *In manus tuas illum, Domine, commendo.*

(Will he do as I asked him — read Psalm 139 every Sunday morning? That's all I asked of

him . . . the only "motherly advice" I offered.
. . . Will he? "In manus tuas — " "Into your
hands, Lord. . . ." You know he won't read
that psalm. Yet you ask.)

Concern, but not nagging worry. Why can't
I sleep? It must be sheer fatigue.

O Night-Listener, why, why should I
have made the choices I've made? Tell me.
. . . One who desires and is given six children should be an extrovert who can coach
and chauffeur, make the dust fly and set out
endless attractive meals with elan, not to mention, carry a community career alongside. She
shouldn't be too small to be divided into so
many people, should she?

Night-Listener, tell me. Why should one to
whom tranquillity, order, are so sweet and who
finds so little of them in this family of five
strapping boys, one youngest girl, and an ab-
sent-minded-professor-husband — why should
she say one day, *Family, let's take a foster
baby!* Or later, when she has read the
medical records of one slightly damaged child:
Yes! . . . Why?

The Yeses of a woman's life. How easy to
say, how hard to fulfill. "Love him . . . honor
and keep him . . . only to him so long as ye
both shall live?" Easy with the scent of orange
blossoms and the long white dress. Easy to say
Yes, Yes, I do, I do. Then the costingness
begins. And what woman, aged forty-four, can

say truly that she has loved and honored and kept herself faithful? In the thousand ways, as well as the one obvious way?

Exactly at the point of deepest cost you see yourself in all your infidelity and you see him who has also been unfaithful — does he know it? — and you say: *For better or for worse!* Right now this is worse than I thought it could be, but it can never be better if I say No. And so you say *Yes. I do.* Again. Every day. Alternative to the Reno of flight.

And you say Yes to the conception of this child, and this . . . and this. (O far-off days when the Sociology profs told you, "You college students should raise big families if you want to do something for humanity; our college-trained people are not reproducing their kind!")

I thought then, I think now — tragic to say No with all of you except the body. To give birth to a child to whom you have said *No* from the beginning. This I have never done. But Yes is easy to say in a moment of fire-flare between two warm bodies. Easy too with childbirth over and a perfect, beautiful child swathed in his delicate shawl.

Beautiful. Yes.

I am sixteen and lying in bed in the tiny room, reading far into the night. I can smell the room still, faintly camphorated, and sense the warmth and texture of the green comforter. But I cannot remember the book except for one phrase about the newborn child resembling "a small hairless monkey."

(After all these years my outrage returns and I am angry with all those who would look upon a newborn child and make crude or casual remarks. . . .)

Our firstborn son lay there like a flower, exquisitely perfect, filled-out, only faintly pink, and his uncle said, "They all look alike," and turned away.

(Dear God, is it not a sin to diminish the joy of another?)

"Beautiful!" When I first looked at you, Latest One who came when I said Yes (when *we* said Yes, *all eight* said Yes) — when I looked at you it was *Beautiful* I called you down inside where the tears are, and where for me they stay. *Yes, Beautiful One*, I said. But now the Yeses are yielding a difficult harvest and I am one weak laborer.

Exactly at the point of deepest cost I see myself. I am forty-four. Shouldn't I be testing the beginnings of a new freedom? The diapered- spoonfed-lullabyed-nosewiped - chauf-feured-coached-summercamped-Six are moving with a certain grace toward adulthood. Haven't I earned a reprieve? Or *something?*

Yes, I tell myself. I've earned the right to go on saying my own Yeses without apology and to carry the consequences of those Yeses without self-pity: Yes to life, Yes to pain, Yes to opportunity, Yes to misfortune, Yes to joy, Yes to tedium, Yes to laughter and the hidden tears, Yes to all those shaky pre-commitments.

Yes, Father, Yes and Always Yes.

Francis of Sales, was it easier for you to say that — and mean it — in your chaste cell? I doubt it. . . .

And when you went out among men and women did those vows of poverty, chastity, and obedience insulate your Yes from corrosion? I've wondered. . . .

Do you know that you helped me to become more womanly, or — how shall I say it? — more accepting of my woman-ness than I had been before I read your *Yes, Father?*

Somehow in those years as I read with infant at breast, you helped me to accept the gay dignity of being a non-specialist, a gatherer of "nosegays." No competition here — let The Professor and his colleagues work with the systems of thought, see things whole, bring wisdom and reason and logic to the task of living. (*He* reads a book and remembers the thesis; *I* read the same book and remember one pungent phrase, one elegant sentence, one sharp insight. . . .) St. Paul and Moses are his. I'm free to trip about gathering flowers from my own wild collection of saints: Underhill, Merton, Lewis, Tillich, Bunyan, Macdonald, Kierkegaard, Dostoevsky, von Hugel, Kelly, Hopkins, Heschel — and from those word-framers of my life, Jesus and David. (Not to mention the saints whose names and book titles are forgotten, but from each of whom I may have plucked that one indestructible flower.)

Strange — I used to quote Walter de la Mare, "Only the rarest kind of best is good enough for the young" — and I chose the books for our young accordingly. But here I am with this collection of phrases plucked from the best, the indifferent, even the really *poor* books devoured in a lifetime of intemperate reading, and they are still shaping, denting, decorating my days.

Picker of seeds, gatherer of flowers — this is what I became, Francis. And I have stored them all in the jumble of my mind, let them fall into the consciousness as they would, accepted the kind of sense they helped to create, the falling petals of intuition. . . . *Yes, Father, Yes and Always Yes.*

In his crib, which is really dangerously shaky (if I speak to the Social Worker will she arrange an allowance for a replacement?), BuBu flails about, changing his position on this hot night. The bed creaks . . . again I am aware of the young child. And I know that I have no choice, really.

Months have passed since that day in the Welfare Office when I sat reading the file of a small boy who did not have much of a chance. It was simple to say Yes then. One can afford to be idealistic for five or six months. ("Five or six months, that's as long as they're asking us to keep him.") I said Yes then. Tonight, in sheer physical fatigue — fatigue so deep that sleep will not come — I say what only a confused, confined, forty-four-year-old mother of six-plus-one can, in the end, say. *Yes, BuBu. God be my witness and bind me to this Yes so long as we both shall live* . . . at least until tomorrow. . . .

From the bedroom I hear The Professor's snoring and, occasionally, the small movements of the child. Having worked through the crazy, difficult ritual of recommitment, suddenly I am relaxed and drowsy. (The peaceful woman who didn't have any peace, after she killed the monster some Peace came on her. . . .) I'll sleep. I can be sure of one thing: BuBu won't awaken me with his crying.

O DAUGHTERS OF JERUSALEM, LET US NOW WEEP FOR THE CHILD WHO KNOWS NOT HOW TO CRY!

"I am against bigness and greatness in all their forms, and with the invisible, molecular forces that work from individual to individual, stealing in through the crannies of the world, like so many soft rootlets, or like the capillary oozing of water, and yet rending the hardest monuments of man's pride, if you give them time."

William James

2

"And
the Child Grew"

The lightning years of my youngmotherhood are fused together and pleasantly blurred. The specifics are recalled only when I read old letters or page through the six fairly-well-kept record books — five blue, one pink — each bearing the title: *Our Baby's First Seven Years.*

I know it's small-potatoes, keeping these records. How could I explain it at the time to my practical busy friends who waxed their floors and made their beds and kept their figures svelte in spite of many small children? How could I tell them why I did it when I hardly knew myself?

I hardly knew . . . yet I must have sensed that what I was doing could become a sort of deposit for each child. The Six grew up knowing Things about themselves — the kinds of things I had wished to know about my own unrememberable years.

O the rainy days, the winter evenings spent

— even in their teens — over those dog-eared repositories! The reappraising of egos, the comparing of statistics, the pride, the fun, of reading the words they had actually said and could never recall saying. . . .

"I don't care much for Mary — she never lets Joseph hold the baby.". . .

"ALL RIGHT. I'll pick it up." And now she breaks into sobs: "But don't say, THAT'S A GOOD GIRL!" . . .

"But how can I be Bigger? I want to do something so I be *bigger*."

"J. J., you can't do a thing about it. Don't you know the Bible says, It is He that has made us and not we ourselves?" (O little five-year-old theologian in the upper-bunk, I'm glad I remembered that one for you. . . .)

But for you, Most Special Child, I've kept no record. They don't make books geared to your kind of growth, and somehow I felt disloyal trying to fit the details of your life into a book like your brothers: I've thought of keeping a daily journal. Daily? No, that would't be fair either.

Living with you, my life's metronome (merrily ticking along at a breathless *presto*) had to be adjusted to *largo*. It's discouraging to keep a record when, day after day, week after week, month after month, there is nothing really new to say. Only in looking back do the landmarks seem clearly defined.

"Stand back and look at the whole," I write in my column. "The particulars, the slowness, the dailiness, the infinitesimal gains and the inevitable backsets, *the loneliness of the long-distance runner* — all these, when concentrated upon, obscure the vision. And *where there is no vision, the people perish* . . . the Little Ones perish too, along with their protectors."

O wild sweet lonely days of our years with you, Thou Littlest. Months pile upon months, and the plateau of your doings seems interminable. There's the simple feat of *locomotion,* which in your brothers and sister we looked upon as an inalienable right, not a gift! But for you the days of the belly-creep stretch into weeks, to months, to a year. Those who watch can picture you "creeping on your belly forever." ("He'll never walk," our children's only grandfather pronounces as he looks at you.) But I am a mother to you and *I Believe.* I don't kid myself into thinking my faith is bottomless. I don't see you winning the mile at the Olympics. I have faith only like that grain of mustard seed. Just enough to see you one day crawling on all fours.

The Significant Person in a child's life, says Fromm, must have faith in that child's possibilities. No false modesty keeps me from admitting it: Right now, Small One, I am the Significant-One in your life. But Faith is so huge a word. Is it really faith to be able to see you only one step ahead of where you now are?

The day comes, beautiful day, when you rock on all fours. Two years old, and ready to creep! Hurrah! A sheepish grin lights up your face, our faces, the room, the world. I don't need to wait those extra months which will certainly pass before you abandon entirely the swimming creep for the swift scampering on all fours. I don't need to wait — I know it will come.

Lord, I believe, help thou mine unbelief.

(Help Thou mine unbelief — for the creeping child of two cannot yet sit alone. . . . He can't sit, but he has somehow discovered the Power of Positive Thinking in regard to doorknobs. He can't sit, he can't stand alone, he can't come close to taking a step, but by sheer will he can reach any doorknob in the house, and we can say good-bye to Peace and Safety.)

Another year passes, and you can execute a wobbly Sit, a rather firm Stand . . . another year — you are nearly four now — and you can take two steps unaided. Steps? Those dreadfully uncoordinated lunges? Yes; for you they are steps, all embroidered with Miracle. Again we project it: we see you walking. Not, perhaps, as any child walks — but walking. There's no timetable to confine our faith. If it happens in a month or six months, a year or two, or more — then *God be praised*. But it will happen.

It does happen. To be five is to walk. With a brace, to be sure, and with a lunge. But upright, as a Person.

As in locomotion, so the pattern repeats itself in other facets of your unfolding personhood. A patternless pattern. There's the miracle of *eating*. Bent over you, those first days you were with us, I found my own mouth puckered in a vain attempt to strengthen your weak sucking reflex; involuntarily I strained to help you get the nourishment you needed. Months . . . years . . . all life in slow motion here, too. A bright day when you first chew your food! Another bright day, a year later, when you insist on independence at the table. Your hold on the spoon, on the cup, is precarious, and when you raise your bowl unsteadily to greedy lips for that last wonderful juicy stuff at the bottom, you miss completely. Days, weeks, months later (How many spilled messes and floor moppings later!) you register full success. Miracle! He's four years old and he can already feed himself.

Then comes the day when I see you kneeling with your dollbaby in your arms, rocking back and forth on your feet, feeding her from your discarded bottle. You grip her for dear-life, gazing into her face with concern at her lack of cooperation. And your own lips, *O Beautiful,* your own lips are puckered in empathy. Full circle.

> (My Mother, come and see what is done because of your love! Because you bent over me, I bent over my child, and now he is bending over *his* child with those same furrows of love and anxiety softening his face.)

When your life is still being measured in months and our faith asks for you only pedestrian responses — the following of object with your eyes; smiling; recognition of family faces — we have not seriously considered music a vital part of your world. Then one night I lean over your crib, head against the rail, weary and forgetful of the ritual. Your strong right hand reaches out to mine, lifts it, drops it, lifts it, drops it, in regular rhythm, while your voice entreats in a persuasive, wordless moan. And so I sing it — your bedtime song: *Hush, Little Baby, don't say a word.* . . . And you smile at your rare success in communication. You smile and beat your hand blissfully on the woolly cover.

And now comes the wild joy of your dancing days. To the tune of your big brother's "Jug-Band Music/ Cert'nly was a tre-eat to me!" you abandon yourself to Rhythm's soul as, dancing on all fours, your head, arms, and legs, all keep the wild but perfect time.

Later there is your insistence upon the Quiet Record at bedtime and naptime, and always your crooning anticipation of the next movement of the symphony before the actual music begins. Where now, Faith? We can't imagine your continued need of music, joy in music. We can't see you leading your Sunday school class, as you surely will do, in a rousing version of "He's got the whole world in His hands."

And the child grew . . . and became strong. First time the therapist at the Rehab Center talks to me about you he tells me that for such children as you, discipline is important. *You must learn to obey,* he says, *like any child.* I look at your rubbery little body lying there on the therapy table. You are almost a year old, yet you can't sit, you can't crawl, you can't cry, you can't do much of anything except flail. How can you do anything *wrong?*

But moments, days, weeks, months, pass. In Abba's arms one day you make a swift, sure grab for the bifocals. In your mother's arms you suddenly reach up and pinch her cheek in — is it really a *loving* vise? And so it begins. . . . Each time (O Days, weeks, months) you make your wild grabs for love or power or possession, we hold you close, loosen your hand by pressure on the wrist (how strong you are!) saying, *Gentle. Gentle.* We straighten your fingers and hold them in a gesture of patting instead of pinching, reaching instead of grabbing. And one day at the first pinch I do not touch your hand, but only say, *Gentle!* and you smile, relax the vise, and pat my cheek.

The pots and pans are now a daily clutter on the kitchen floor. We don't say *No,* for you need pots and pans, and ours are all old, baby-battered. But months pass and you learn what to do when I say, *Put them back, please. . . . Fine! Back on the shelf. . . . That's where they belong! Thank you! . . .* endlessly.

(I defy heaven and earth to describe the rasping, fingernails-on-chalkboard tension of standing by, watching, waiting, while that uncoordinated body of yours makes the excruciating effort to do what the Significant Person in your Life asks you to do. An ache spreads across my chest and my arms are heavy with wanting to help. But I move about my work, merely encouraging, smiling, as the little successes appear, insisting when they don't, helping only when it is obvious that I have asked too much.) Now they're all in — never mind how. After your nap they'll be out again, and the process will repeat, repeat for days, weeks, months, years on end. You'll be playing with pots and pans for a long time. . . .

You have your own shelf of raggle-taggle books, but months drag by until you can respond when I say, "No, *your* books are on *your* shelf. . . . These are Abba's — put them back. . . . These are Mamma's — put them back. . . . *Your* books are on *your* shelf." Yet the time does come, and you do respond with the shy grin and the obedient attention to the bottom shelf. In the meantime you glow from the praise you receive when you push back the books you have pulled out of their places on the shelves above your shelf. You glow, you shine! And now the obsession of your life for weeks on end seems to be: Keep pulling them out so they'll say, *Put them back!* Keep putting them back so they'll say, *Thank you! Big Fellow! Right!*

"Shall we sin more that grace might more abound?" You answer it with a resounding *Yes*.

Your first temper-tantrum. . . . We recall that for your brothers and sister this milestone was the occasion for a quick unemotional, but stinging, spanking. Over the years this had seemed to be the best solution for us; it was quick and easy and, in the case of those six, it was effective after only one or two tries. But physical pain leaves you unmoved. You can't cry; even a sharp bump from a fall brings only a whimper from you. A smack on the hand which has reached out to touch the hot stove, makes you giggle and flex the fingers. So what to do, when you make those power grabs for the coffee pot, the electric fan, the stereo; when

I restrain you and you throw a small tantrum? In the urgency of the moment I'm not always wise enough to have an alternative activity for you, and you are not always reasonable enough to take it.

Then one day I do what I have done only rarely to our other children, and always hated myself for (believing, as I do, that the face is *the person* more than any part of the body and should not be violated). Only in anger had I done it to them. I am not angry now, but I give you a tiny smack on your cheek. You look at me amazed and — I swear it — respectful. The tantrum is over before it has gotten a good start, and you climb into my arms, crowing happily.

Otto, your therapist at the Rehab Center, would approve, I think — even if I don't, quite. But it is only the beginning of pitting will against will, of guiding where you do not wish to go but must learn to go; of refusing to be a victim or let you be a victim of your handicaps; of letting you pick yourself up when you fall, unless you are really hurt; of channeling, insisting, permitting, yet never losing faith that no effort is lost.

It is only the beginning of refusing to be overcome with pity when you hug with arms, legs, teeth, with your whole You as I lean over your crib to lay you in it. There is gentle disengagement, sweet talk and singing, but you are not allowed, not ever, to win out in the Bedtime Battle. Days, weeks, months — and one night you willingly accept the bondage. You even make the urgent asking noises and the pointing to indicate that you want us to put on your night-splint which is meant to correct the inward-rotation of your feet, but which keeps you a prisoner in your crib.

The battle, we know, isn't over. Your strong will is bound to persist, and bound to bring confrontation. But you *will* respond to people who keep their cool when you lose yours. Otto *is* pleased, months later, when you begin regular therapy sessions with him. He's not a man to praise easily. But he does say that you are an exceptional child. He does say that too many of the physically handicapped kids who come to him are so undisciplined he can do little with them. You, he says, are cooperative and obedient; responsive without being overly submissive. "He's got a mighty strong will that isn't broken — and we don't want it to be," explains Otto. "We want him to be able to defy, to say no, to stand his ground; but he's learning something else important: there are times when we have to bend."

That day the Significant Person in your life leaves the Rehab Center giddy, singing. She can't wait to tell Abba, the kids. . . . She doesn't think of the long road that led to this day, nor the long road stretching ahead.

37

Quite suddenly, she realizes that she too is reaping a fruit of discipline. All those years when the Six were small, she would fall into bed each night, sick with the seventy-times-seven breaches of her patience. Strange — she hasn't thought about patience for a long time. In fact, it's been months since she has felt the pangs of chronic impatience. This new measure of freedom from that particular bondage, she sees now, is your gift to her. O, not a perfect gift, not entire, not everlasting. But a substantial gift . . . a very usable gift.

So you are learning discipline and I am learning patience in the same school.

"Will he learn to talk, do you think?" people asked.

"Of course! He'll learn to talk — in time." Did I really believe it? And would I have been more anxious about your not talking if you had been my born-child? Maybe so. And maybe I cared more than I thought, for in those early years when your speech took the form of pointing, pantomime, demanding noises, eloquent eyes, I wrote in my column:

> Last night I had this vivid dream in which he crawled to me, smiled up at me, and enunciated his first halting, recognizable words. Then quickly gaining momentum, he was rattling off the names of everything within sight! It was one of those wonder-

fully exhilarating dreams — the kind that leaves a person with a residue of faith and hope even after awakening. BuBu will talk, I know, in his own time.

The "residue of faith and hope" has a chance to wear pretty thin before the day comes when you reward it with that first uncoordinated, spasmodic opening and closing of the fingers of your good right hand to say good-bye, good night, closely followed by the syllable anyone can recognize (well, *we* can!) as "Bye-bye."

Months later there comes an electrifying moment when you touch the oven door and give us the incomparable gift of your first real word: *Hah*. Two years later, at age five, your vocabulary is fairly bursting the seams of that threadbare faith and hope. A dozen words! A three-word sentence! (Dear God, how can I explain it all so that people will know a miracle has come to pass? A very special five-year-old is insisting, "Help Mamma clean!")

The funny little imitations that give us pleasure today remind me of your beginnings as a *social creature*. Here is this lump of an infant who has come to us with only the most basic of responses, who even now, after several months with us, does not smile or follow us with his eyes. Yet a new voice, a foreign presence in the house, keeps you from sleeping, from eating, even if you remain in your crib, back in the bedroom.

But however tentative your reaching out to strangers, the passing weeks and months find you ever more firmly addicted to your family — to Abba, those ridiculous boys, the beloved sister. With more months, years, you come to welcome the regulars who come and go in our home . . . the Mary who cleans and irons; the "other Mary" who eats with us once a week; Becky, your sister's friend and yours too. And you show us all that you like being in our world. You show us as any child does — by imitation. What does it matter if the time-schedule is off a year or two? Or more?

So long ago that there's a haze settling over the month and year of its happening, you make it plain to us that you mean to join the human race. . . . Abba (that One in your life who is daily becoming a more Significant Person to you) accuses me wrathfully: "You've *got* to stop holding the pins in your mouth when you diaper this boy." I wrathfully reply that never in my life have I EVER EVER EVER put a diaper pin in my mouth, and I don't intend to do it now. But somebody has — someone who cared for this child while I had my last brief vacation. And now, day after day after day you *will* make a grab for those pins and try to get them into your mouth, to hold them as a special favor to the one who is going to all this bother for the sake of your comfort! You *will* insist on being like the people you love. . . .

But growth in the subtler imitations is evident too. When the pins are gone, you reach to give me another, imaginary pin — but this one is given with a difference. This time you smile that sheepish, embarrassed smile indicating that you are pulling a leg.

There's a Sunday afternoon when the creeping three-year-old clambers onto the sofa with a book (Well, everyone else is reading — why shouldn't he?) But look! the book is upside-down. What to do? Amazing discovery — an up-side-down book can be changed to right-side-up. You make that change, and you glow, even before we praise.

And now the imitations come faster and faster. You iron and clean like Mary, put your feet up like Tim, comb your hair like James. No more eating from a highchair tray, but from the table, like Family. Fold hands to pray, sing the rollicking birthday song with the brothers, clap with the TV audiences over the inane humor.

And, believe me, you know — better than many adults — the attitude of Worship wherever you encounter it, no matter what the words. Eating alone one morning, you can overhear the TV in the next room. Suddenly you fold your hands and drop your brown head almost into your cereal as you hear the children and Miss Suzy on *Romper Room* go into their chant: "I pledga-a leegunce to-tha flag. . . ."

Remember the child who never cried? It's true that you still don't cry in the manner of most children when hurt or angry — those outraged, prolonged sirens of noise. But there is a day when your lower lip first juts out in response to hurt feelings, and a few real tears run down your cheeks. You swipe at them in wonder with your flailing arm. Tears. A new experience. Tears. How wonderful — you couldn't know.

Watching you learn to cry, a process of years, convinces me again that one of the silliest of the many silly things we teach children about "Little Lord Jesus" is this line — "no crying He makes." *That little Jewish baby did cry!* And you, my Love, you, Our Love, you too are learning to cry. You too, like "Little Lord Jesus," are *human!* I repeat those words with Holy Laughter as I watch you stand at the door, as I hear you filling the house with a screaming wail. . . . Your beloved Abba, briefcase in hand, is going down the walk to his office, leaving you behind, and you are . . . *crying*.

The child grew. You grow . . . and grow . . . and you will keep growing beyond the bounds of our faith. So the days are filled with surprises rather than disappointments. No one within your charmed circle says as he looks at you, "What are *normal* three-and-one-half-year-olds doing now? *Normal* five-year-olds?" We have forgotten if we ever knew, or it has simply become irrelevant. If we ask, we ask only as does Dr. Sobol at the Crippled Children's Clinic: "What is he doing now that he did not do last time we saw him?"

No one you love, none who loves you has set a timetable for you, and so you are one of the freest of God's children to walk the earth. And in giving you this freedom, we have learned something of what it is to be free ourselves.

O FREEDOM . . . O FREEDOM . . . !

The visitor glances uncomfortably at the Child, then at the mother. "I . . . I really don't know how to go about trying to relate to Them," she admits.

"O, it's quite simple," the mother smiles, "**Look** at him; **speak** to him; **touch** him as you would touch any child. In short -- just treat him as if you were what he is -- A Human Being."

3

"Kiss Not the Son
While
The Orphan Stands By"

The fires of life diminish in different people at
different rates, I suppose — the fires of
idealism, enthusiasm, wonder, productivity. . . .
I know women of my age — this catch-all of an
age, neither young nor old — who are
vigorous, busy, wiry, and fiery. *Hustlers,* my
mother's people called them. It was supposed to
be a high compliment. But no one ever said it
of me. I can face it now, in these middle-years
— what I could never quite accept earlier: I am
really a peasant — a reflective peasant, to be
sure — and I'm not going to fly after all, just
plod. Without brilliance and the dedication to
Excellence which brilliance often inspires, I'm
not going to make that splotch of brightness in
the world after all. That's not self-pity, it's just
realism, I tell myself. I tell myself further that
I am content — even happy — to admit it.

And with that dream of adding some un-
forgettable brightness, the Gracious-Living bit

has evaporated, too. Strange — when did these preoccupations cease to nag?

I can remember flinging a hand around our living room and complaining ruefully to a friend, "It's not that I really *mind* living with other people's replaced furniture. It's just that I'd like my house to say something about *me* — and that means I'd have to choose what I put into it!" (Why were people always offering us stuff — was it the family-size, or some mystique of vulnerability that clings to us? Probably the latter — where is there a family of eight such suckers? People who never sold *anything* at a profit; parents who somehow didn't realize that families need savings accounts; kids who couldn't even sell a Brownie cookie or a Parkside rose without flinching?)

The dreams have gone, but perhaps better than brightness, better than gracious living, are these beginnings of self-understanding. . . . For now I see that my house *does* reflect me. It's furnished with bits and pieces of people I've loved, just as my mind is furnished with bits and pieces of the books I've loved. . . .

There's the bookcase — a leftover from the *Christian Living* office. Needs painting again, but it's sturdy after twenty years of being the most important piece in our living room, whether on the Hill or on the Corner. . . . That sofa, true, it needs to be camouflaged (it's not worth reupholstering) but it's a bearer of

grace, somehow, because of Alan and Eleanor
. . . the table from the secondhand basement
of the furniture store — I'll never replace it,
even though I can't use my lovely Chinese
linen place mats on its battered veneer top.
Evelyn passed it by so that I could buy it at a
time when we needed a table — any table —
and had little to invest. The china cupboard
that was their bookcase . . . Mary's record
cabinet . . . the bed that Anna and Frank
slept in for twenty-five years, and we slept in
for twenty-five more . . . the roomy, dated
Wenger dresser . . . the bulky old desk that
was D. K.'s rolltop. . . . No "period" harmony
here; no furniture-store-window correctness;
no *Better Homes and Gardens* luxury . . . not
one really beautiful piece except most beautiful
to us, the walnut corner table loved into being
by a young son. . . .

But now I see it. My house *has* been
furnished by my choices. I chose to accept what
was given when we needed it. I chose to keep
it, years later, when I could have asked Abba
for new things, and he would have given
them. . . . It *is* me, all of it. And I like it.
Dear God, I do like it.

And if I've surrendered that dream of adding a brightness to the world, still, I have been
given graces. One of them is that I have learned
to love children of my flesh and not of my flesh,
to love them — I think — more or less open-

handedly. And hopefully.

Even as I write this, the Nightmare recurs: *I am suddenly incapacitated or killed. He is suddenly removed from all that is loved and familiar. Removed to what? To whom?*

I've loved my church — I've lived my entire life in its context. But lately I'm perplexed. The adjective *Christian,* so glibly tossed about, bothers me. The noun as well. I shrink from using a word that has become a label for the good, the easy, the successful, the *indifferent* life. (Yes, Mr. Rollo May — I believe all you say about the opposite of love being not hate but indifference!)

The people of my church — they believe it's good to care about homeless children, yet how few care for any but their own children in their own homes! They give more than their share of money and goods to the poor; they involve themselves in all sorts of short-term, intermittent goodnesses and long-term, planned goodnesses.

But few of them appear to make commitments which will really change or constrict their style of life — *a very comfortable style of life, really,* in spite of the murmurs one hears about high prices and low salaries. (After all, how can we make room for another person, however desperate his situation, when the children need their teeth straightened?)

And I'm afraid — terribly afraid — that if the Day of Nightmare should come for me (or for people like me) there would be no one to come forward and receive this child . . . that he would be shunted from foster home to indifferent foster home, or that he would end his days — he and those like him — in one of those Places where the light would go out of the happy eyes, the bright hair would dull, the quick responses dwindle, and the Good People here would forget that there ever was a little boy like him, lunging about in the corridors of the Big Round Church.

And I know that my own cry is an echo of the cry of every parent of a Special Child. *Would anyone — if not for the child's sake, if not for my sake — would anyone even for Jesus' sake love this child who is so special?*

Sometimes, like today, when Abba asks me testily why I don't choose a project and see it through, why I am always saying wistfully that I wish I could do one thing really well, yet neglect doing what *he* thinks I do well. Sometimes I fight a scream to all earth and heaven to listen to my grievances. If this one who is supposed to be closest to me has not understood my goals, my conflicts, what the days demand of me, then what understanding is there for me anywhere? I fight a wild scream against all the THEYS who seem pitted against me in my struggle to carry out my commitments with freedom and integrity.

He goes off to write in his air-conditioned private office. The only impediment to his work will be, perhaps, a colleague stopping in to chew a little fat. (Oh for a colleague to stop in — just once a week, even, to tell me about a book she's read, a thought she's developed, an insight that has burst in upon her! I'd even settle for weather-talk, or that most-boring-of-all talk — dieting, or the price of food. . .) *He* is bitter toward me this morning because of my "unproductivity" and *I* am bitter against him because he cannot see the true nature of my investment!

I remember the days when I thought parts of the psalms should be ripped from the Bible. Such bitterness, such pathological self-pity — as if the whole world were lined up against the singer-of-songs! A friend suggested that one should read these psalms with the understanding that the "enemies" are one's own enemies of the spirit. *Pride* and all that. What a resourceful explanation, I thought then. But now I know that the psalmist's enemies were not just spiritual enemies. And now I know that it was *right* for him to scream out his hatred against them. Who can speak his love that has not spoken his hatreds?

The powers of THEM against me and against all I am trying to do! Dear God! (*All* I am trying to do? Face it, Woman — you're not doing *that* much. You know personally several of those Super-women who, though they have big families of their own, still care for a half-dozen foster children, and do it with a flair!) True, I'm doing what I deeply *want* to do. Why then blame and complain?

I cry out, I blame, I complain not because the task itself is so heavy. The heaviness is the heaviness of *Them* — of all who do not share my joy, who do not attempt to understand, who "dim wonder by indifference," who look without seeing.

Take — the joy of watching a child slowly, slowly grow from a pasty mound of flesh to responsive brightness. Take — the joy of seeing, in retrospect, each step of the process; seeing it and knowing that without you, without your family's love, acceptance, attention, this flower might never have bloomed. You want to go out and stand on the street corner and yell with John Woolman, "My friend, do you know Grace!" Look! Look and see what can happen! Be glad with me over this little saved lamb!

It should be enough to know that a very few children, having been put into my care, are thriving, and should — hopefully — be influences for good in a sorry world. Not geniuses, not statesmen or churchmen — but surely salt and light, in small ways, on little hills. It should be enough to know that one Special Child in the world is likely to have received, whatever the outcome of his life, more joy and fullness than he would have without us. And mostly I'm content to know this.

But on days like today . . . I cry out against the intolerable burdens laid on by *Them*. *They* are the ones who infer that you could do more good writing or teaching or working in an office — anything other than caring for one "defective" child.

They are the judges and planners of other people's lives; one of them actually tells you that, frankly, you aren't as interesting as you used to be, and you should free yourself of the child — this child she has not even bothered to learn to know. . . .

They are the veddy-rich mother of two who remarks, "I'M SURE IT'S WONDERFUL — what you're doing, but I don't see how you can do it without neglecting your own children." And, "It's not as if the child were *born* to you in that condition. You have a choice."

I have a choice? Dear God, she says I have a choice!

They are the ones who stare in the supermarkets; strange, how on days like this the one who smiles gently at the Little Feller just doesn't make up for the nine who stare coldly.

They are the ones whose first words on seeing this Child-That-Is-Loved are: *Will they be able to do anything about straightening his eyes?* Or, *Is he toilet-trained?*

(Someday, someday, I swear I shall say to one of *Them:* "Will the doctors be able to do anything about *your* child's enormous ears?" "Hasn't *your* baby learned not to cry when he's hungry?")

They are the ones whose second question is: *How long do you expect to keep him? They get more difficult as they grow older, you know.* At such times — so far — I've managed to keep the bitter reply in check, answering, "A day at a time." Or, "Indefinitely." Or, "As long as he needs us — as long as we can take care of him, I suppose." But I warn you, *They.* I warn you. One day I will ask you in return: "How long do you expect to be a mother to your child? How long do you plan to be a wife to your husband? How long do you expect to keep *your* covenants?"

They are the adults who enter our home and act as if we have no child. They see our pictures and our books, our table settings and our food. But they do not see the Child.

They are the telephone mechanic who draws back when That Boy makes a happy noise to see him work with his tools — how he does love tools! As the mechanic leaves, he asks dryly, "Wotsamatter with it?" There you have it. This one at least is frank. And in his frankness he focuses on the one terrible wounding fact of the matter: the *Theys* about whom I silently scream, who on days like this make a burden of what should be a joy — they deny him his very personhood, making of him an *It*.

They are the friend who tells me about the day her family was picnicking, and some retarded children moved into the picnic area. "My children came to me," she recalled, "and said, *Let's get out of here.* And we agreed; it was eerie."

This dear woman could weep to hear me read to her the first tentative chapters of my proposed book about The Child; and then question my use of a title which would reflect badly on Jesus, she thought, since some people might misunderstand and think I was inferring that *He* was retarded. (Strange — she believes that Jesus "carried her sins," yet it apparently never occurred to her that if Jesus would do that, He would be the last to worry about being identified with My Beloved Son!)

They are the one you had counted on for understanding, who sympathizes (who wants sympathy?) "It must make you sad to think what a *normal* child his age is doing now." Or another who admits he's not convinced that "defectives" should be allowed to live. . . .

They are the preachers to whom a retarded

child is mainly a sermon illustration of the tragedy of stunted spiritual growth.

They are the mournful ones who believe that the worst that can befall a family is to have a "defective child" — far worse than to have a child who turns out to be a blah conformist or even a moral defective. "We don't care if it's a girl or a boy — just so it's normal," they say in our presence.

They are the naive ones who say, "Somebody told me they think you folks love that child as if he were your own! Remarkable!" Or, "It's amazing how everyone in the family seems to love him — even more than if he were normal!"

They are the aging grandfather who writes dryly, "Yes, I remember him. So he had an operation? What wonders me is why they want to throw away their money on people like him, the shape he's in."

> O My Mother of the gentle eyes, the long-fingered, supple hands (you always held your hand on my forehead when I would throw up; sometimes I can still feel its pressure . . .), what would *you* have written to me about BuBu's surgery?

And there is this one — Dear God, will I ever forget? Do I *want* to forgive? The Little Guy has a nose for such a person, and ordinarily he wouldn't touch him. But he's pushing this

55

chair around — such fun, when you can't walk alone! — and the Big Man is standing in his way. He tentatively takes hold of the Man's hand to entreat him to move. Big Man shakes off the small hand as if it were the hand of a leper, then looks furtively from side to side to see if anyone has observed him. . . .

The child tries again. This time, when the hand is shaken off the child loses his balance and falls with his heavy brace. Again the eyes of the Big Man shift to and fro to see if anyone has observed his Smallness. . . . *And so great is his aversion and fear, he cannot even help the child to his feet.*

I look at him, at his own small, perfect child, and I want to stride up to him and say softly, carefully (ever-so-softly, ever-so-carefully), "The little boy won't hurt you —" But in my outrage I cannot even move. And I hate myself for that silence. And I hate him more than I have hated anyone, ever.

Abba says to me, on the way home, "He should be pitied, not hated." I say to Abba, *You pity him; I'll hate him.*

Abba throws back his head and roars. He always laughs when Mother Bear — as he puts it — gets up on her hind legs to defend one of her cubs. He always laughs. And tonight I hug The Child in the darkness and laugh too. And cry.

"*Not* while the orphan stands by!" warns the

proverb. Yet THEY, in the presence of the unmarried flaunt their marriedness, holding hands, caressing in that obvious, unfree manner that says: *He's mine, I own him!* Or protests overmuch, *See, you other women cannot tempt me — I'm an attentive husband!*

(Dear God, I have enough stupidities; thanks for sparing me this piddling jealousy . . . and thanks for a man who sees other women, has always seen other women, as persons, not as sex-objects . . . who can greet his female friends and mine with kisses if he feels like it — and who is not threatened by my doing the same with our friends who happen to be men.)

They flaunt their marriedness, they fly the banner of parenthood before those to whom parenthood has been denied, or who have chosen to deny themselves of it. . . . They think it's wonderful (odd?) that there are people who *can* care about the orphan . . . and they go on kissing the son and showering him with gifts and privileges beyond his need, beyond his desiring, beyond his good.

They have said to me: But you didn't bargain to keep him past babyhood. Why should you feel responsible? (Had the child been *born* to us, would they say, "But you bargained for a *healthy* baby; you can't throw your life away for a child barely human"?)

And I have said, True . . . I didn't know. And

if I *had* known, I would have lacked the courage. I didn't know to what I was committing myself. Neither did I, when I set out to take the Jesus-way seriously, long ago. Nor when I took marriage vows. Nor when each of our children was born to us, did I think to say, "I will do so much and no more."

They ... They ... They. ...

They are "nice good Christian people." My friends. Yesterday I could listen to their artless words concerning Our Son Our Chosen One, and smile indulgently, "Father, forgive them for they know not!" But today? Not today. I hate them. I do not *blame* them, but I hate them all with a Perfect Hatred.

They are nice good Christian people. But they are my friends-turned-enemy; and times like today I hate them with deep hatred because they make it difficult for me to carry out my commitment with joy. *And the good* (says my friend Abraham Joshua Heschel) *without the joy is a good half-done.*

I hate them most because — bitter knowledge — *They* are myself when I find myself saying, "This is our foster child," and not "This is Our Son." I hate myself for it and weep — inside — all kinds of Peter's-tears over the denial. ...

My great hatred makes me lonely. My feet drag to the Big Church. I should tell someone. My pastor? A friend? What pastor? What friend?

No, I won't tell. I don't want them to think me peevish, small — which I am. After all, IT IS A WONDERFUL WORK YOU ARE DOING WITH THIS CHILD. Why burst the bubble and show them my contempt for all — including myself — who "love humanity and can't stand people."

I read the psalms of hate again, and I see David's pattern, I think: a statement of trust in God . . . a burst of wild hatred . . . a restatement of trust. I read my own psalm again and I am perplexed. Well, at least I have said my hatred. The thing is finished.

Finished? The end of my hatred of *Them* has joined the beginning of my self-hatred; the end of my self-hatred has joined the beginning-again of my hatred of *Them*. The circle is complete. A vicious circle.

And now Something Else is indicated. Something Other is needed. O God. . . .

O GOD O GOD O GOD

"If you are penitent, you love. And if you love, you are of God. All things are atoned for, all things are saved by love. Love is such a priceless treasure that you can redeem the whole world by it, and expiate not only your own sins but the sins of others."

Dostoevsky

4

"A Child
That Is Loved . . ."

Today I am forty-six. When I was eleven
and *my* mother was forty-six, that great age
was equivalent to one foot in the grave.

To a young mother in her twenties, forty-
six represented ripe middle age.

Toward my middle thirties I could look at a
woman of forty-six without pitying her.

Now I note with relief that one authority
calculates middle age to begin around fifty-five.

But today . . . today . . . *I don't know*. Today
I feel in the bones that it's hardly likely I'll
see thirty more birthdays, let alone forty-six.
Our family doesn't run to longevity.

My Mother, I'm trying today to recreate
your forty-sixness. And you are not here to
help me. I have so many questions —
questions I wasn't ready to ask until after
you were gone. I want to know how you
think I'm doing?

Dean Bender used to say: If a man is not better than his father he is not as good as his father. . . .

Am I as good as you were?

I know what you'd say. . . .

That day I went through your pitiful pile of possessions with the brothers and sisters (How proud we all were that you left so little!) and came upon The Box, that day I sensed what you would say if you were here and I asked you (Oh, it would be a joke to both of us) my stupid question. . . . There in that box were all the articles, every bit of verse I'd ever had published — little of which I'd cared for enough to keep. But you cared — the care was blazing in the neatly cut edges, the tidy arrangement within the box.

And that was the moment when the whole weight of a death-shattered relationship struck me.

You would say now, "Honey-Dear —" (*Honey-Dear* — how redundant it sounds, how oversweet, coming from anyone but you; but from you it was right — it was your motherword) "Honey-Dear, I'm proud of you."

But you were hopelessly prejudiced in your children's favor. And you never did know how good a person you were. . . .

No, I'm not as good as my mother. . . .

Another thing. I haven't really learned much in all these years. The first twenty years — that aware childhood, that lovely-difficult adolescence — I was madly, freely testing the senses. But the next twenty! Dear God, what happens to make us succumb to that imperious piety of Answer-giving?

And now I've been asking a few questions.

As a young Thing I had viewed people in their forties as Pillars who had arrived at staunch convictions, a sure sense of direction, a fixed integrity. So here I am, less sure than ever of those neat answers. Still ambivalent. Still questioning.

Why, for instance, can't I do what I've chosen to do without this periodic reevaluation, recommitment? Why do I sense that Elizabeth Browning's little verse was written for me, yet feel defensive about all the dreams of mine that died along the way to this discovery?

> I was too ambitious in my deed
> And thought to distance all men in success,
> Till God came on me, marked the place,
> and said,
> "Ill-doer, henceforth keep within this line,
> Attempting less than others" — and I stand
> And work among Christ's little ones, content.

Strange . . . saying it again reminds me that in spite of the introspective Whys, the slow maturation, the ambivalence — I am really, deeply, content. In spite of the lapses when I compare my life with that of my freer peers (freer?), I know that the way I've chosen — even inadvertently chosen — is freeing. And if I haven't learned to live according to the Gracious-Living pattern; if at forty-six I'm still gauche and erratic, still asking questions about faith and existence; if I'm still changing my mind — So? Is it so dreadful to be human?

At least I know something of what it means to have *Joy*. And *Freedom*.

At least I've come to believe firmly two or three things. (Remember when we were urged to be able to definitively explain and defend *what we believe?*) The guilt over my utter inadequacy to carry out this task is gone. . . .)

> *I believe in Grace*. ("My friend, do you know Grace?")
> *I believe in Love*. (Love is of God, God is Love, and whoever loves knows God, whether or not he knows that he knows God.)
> *I believe that nothing done or given in Love is ever lost*.

Child so costing and so giving, what have you done to me? To us all?

We knew this radiant gentleman who asked us, years ago when Small Joyce was living with us: "But why didn't you take an older child instead of an infant — one you could teach about Jesus? To have a baby for only a year — then everything is lost!"

Dear God, I wanted to say to him, I should have said to him, "How can any child of ten 'learn to love Jesus' if no one has ever loved *him*?"

Joyce of the black curls and blue eyes and fair skin — who went from us back into squalor and carelessness, to a mother-that-was-no-mother and a grandmother who hated the sight of you! They told us you'd be adopted, so we released you with joy. But when she came to get you (the Social Worker with the hard eyes and always the stale aura of cigarettes clinging to her), she announced triumphantly that they had finally persuaded your mother-that-was-no-mother to take you back.

"You know," she simpered, *"in the end it is the natural mother who is best for the child."*

And you, Happy Elf, in your pink-checked dress, you waved Bye all sparkles, all shine. You didn't know where you were going, you who, from the time you were three weeks old, had known nothing but gentle voices, laughter, joyous roughhousing.

I'm no weeper (I find it impossible to listen sympathetically to the cliche, "I just couldn't keep a foster child — I'm too tenderhearted to ever be able to take a child, then give it up!") I'm no weeper. But I remember that sunny

August morning eight years ago when I stood in the dusty drive on The Hill, and all around, within, without was pain and blur. But even while I turned to go back into the noisy household I was telling you silently: "We've done all we could for you. You won't remember your first parents. Your life, it appears, will be cruel, hard, unfair. But maybe it'll be easier — a little easier, because of this lovely first year. Nothing we've given you, surely, will be lost. . . ."

(Fat little girl, where are you now, and what has Love done for you? I ask it, but I don't need to know. *I believe in Love.*)

I *do* believe in Love in spite of the psalms of hatred to which I've at rare times succumbed. And I'm not alone, though at times I've wailed to a forgetful God, a mindless fellow-man, that *I only I am left alone in all Israel!* And this Child Our Son — what would he have been without Love? (Face it, Woman, not just *your* love —) All the joy, fun, excitement, encouragement, discipline, of life with Abba, brothers, sister. All the friendliness and commendation and exclamation of friends, neighbors, relatives, passing guests, and the street children.

And now the love-psalms take over as they document one by one those miracles of acceptance, interaction, insight, illumination, affirmation — the results of one Special Child's involvement in a family, a community. ·

The honeymooners return. They glow from their Colorado trek. But the report of the trip must wait. Within minutes of their arrival she is engrossed in the hugs of the Little Feller. (His vocabulary holdings are still meager enough to be listed on five fingers, but they do include the name of the Beloved Anne — which comes out now, over and over, as "Ahhhhhhhn!") Seconds later more delighted yips emerge from the living room where the new husband is lying on his back, tumbling over the floor with his fearless, relaxed small brother. . . .

A stranger stops in with his girl, a friend of ours. The Small Guy gazes, puzzled. Then, with a glad cry, he lunges toward him, grabbing him fiercely about the knees. The poor young fellow doesn't know how to receive this affection — nor do we know *why* he's receiving it. Until . . . until we look again at his profile, his hair, his coloring. An easy mistake for so small child to make, after so long a time. For this One *does* resemble the big brother who used to come in from his college classes and swing The Squirt up on his shoulders for a high ride through the house. (High enough to reach up at the arch and put those grimy finger marks where Mamma doesn't like them to be!) But that was long ago — before he went away on that train. And now the perplexed Bu-Bu sees his mistake. Of course this isn't the one. Otherwise why does he stand so still and look so funny. If it were Jon they'd be all messed up with each other by now!

The high school senior labors over his college entrance application. There's a place for brothers and sisters. I look over his shoulder and read the list: *five* brothers, one sister, with names and ages. It hasn't even occurred to this one that the youngest brother is not legally a brother. It hasn't occurred to him to insert "foster." I go away without pointing out his mistake. (Actually the mistake is mine — why *shouldn't* he include the name of the child who in every important sense of the word, is, indeed, his brother?)

J. B. stops me on the street to say, "I met your daughter the other day. . . . She was pulling The Boy in his wagon. She seemed so proud of him — introduced him to me as her little brother. *I liked that.*" Inside, I'm singing.

"When will we adopt him, Mom?" A gangling teenager, slouching against the cupboard, after-school sandwich in hand, is troubled. He flares, "But *I'd hate it*. It's not fair to be in our family and have a different name. . . ." Months pass and the same awkward fellow confides, "I'm worried, Mom." It finally comes out: He's worried about our proposed Sabbatical next year. He listens to our planning sessions, and we keep talking of going without the Little Guy. What will happen to him?

"That's no way to treat him! You wouldn't do that to your own child!" I stoutly explain that indeed we would, if the child were special in the way that this one is special. A trip like this would be even more difficult for him than for us. And once we got to Israel, what about a school? No Aux Chandelles, where he could continue to learn and develop among children who speak his language, and teachers who understand that language. . . . No Dr. Sobol, who has followed his case from the beginning, performed surgery on his leg, prescribed his braces which make walking possible. Besides, I go on, we plan to do a lot of tramping-about en route. How would he manage that? In a burst of loyalty he explodes hotly, "I'd carry him on my back!"

The tall high-schooler with the shock of wheaty hair is responsible for the lesson in his Sunday school class. He has an idea, and he prepares the lesson accordingly. But he is hardly prepared for the response when, taking his little brother in tow, he sits in the circle of his school friends discussing what it means to have such a child in one's home. Another class drifts in, then another, having heard interesting sounds through the partitions. . . . He comes home radiant: "He was great — he just loved those kids — went around shaking hands with the boys and kissing the girls! But the nicest thing," he adds, "was that *they* liked *him* so much. You just feel warmer toward your friends when they like a kid like him." *Yes,* I think, *you do.*

But the story is not ended. The contagion spreads. The Intermediate Department asks for a chance to hear about BuBu and Life with BuBu. Then the Primary Department. And because one tall fellow loves his friends and his brother, the miracles of acceptance are multiplied, and now there are at least a hundred kids in the Big Round Church who know that this bespectacled oddity is a Human Being. Once they may have avoided the lurching Little Guy, or even feared him. Now they realize he may be more like them than he is different from them. He is a lovable person who gives and receives, rejects and accepts, feels, responds.

The documentation of love is not exhausted by the family context. Tom and Steve perform their rituals of handshaking and greeting with their friend whenever they pass his outdoor playyard. After he has outgrown that confinement, they patiently answer his endless, "What you doin'?" as he watches them paint the house, husk the corn, trim the lawn. . . . Our Thursday-night friend is greeted by cries of welcome, great knee-tackling hugs.

He knows, this canny guy, which guest will

welcome, which will avoid him or be unaware of
his friendly advances. The latter he will ignore. Well, *usually* he'll ignore them. Except in
the face of sheer necessity, as when Abba
and a friend sit in deep theological discussion,
unaware that a small boy is having difficulty
with a truck. The child reaches for the hand
of the stranger — it's lying right there on the
arm of the chair, so why not?

What he doesn't realize is that this is the
hand of another Absent-minded-Professor like
Abba. . . . The hand dangles, as the theological
discussion continues. The boy looks up in
wonder, tugging again at the hand. No response. Resignation pulls his face into a droop
as he gently lifts the big hand, placing it back
on the arm of the chair . . . and the theological
discussion goes on without a break. With an I-
should-have-known-better-air, the unfortunate
trucker calls for Mamma, who has been smirking
in the wings. . . .

But not all professors are absent-minded.
Love remembers long, long ago when the
child could only "swim" on the floor. The Yale
Doctor, sitting in the wicker chair — again,
deep in a theological discussion with Abba —
merely looks at the child on the floor.

What is in that look to make the baby
crow with happiness? As if it is the simplest
and most natural thing in the world for him
to do, with no comment, the brilliant man

71

scoops up the child, and this baby who up to now has shied from any stranger, spends the rest of the discussion blissfully settled in Jonathan's arms. (Not everyone that *says*, Love, Love. . . .)

Love remembers and remembers and remembers. . . .

Love remembers the folksinger visiting in our home, the one whose songs are woven into the texture of this family's life, whose records of songs and dances from the Kentucky mountains are an integral part of each child's growing-up memories. . . . Yet now she will be remembered by this woman for her stroking of a baby's head and crying out, "What beautiful hair!"

Love remembers our favorite rabbi — not only for the brightness shining from his face, the affection spilling out in words and letters and welcoming hugs; not only for the quick mind, the caring, the pride in his Jewishness, his Pearl, his fine children. But also — and now mainly — for the lively joy in that face as he looked on our child again and again during that visit, looked on him and noted the "lovely light in his eyes."

Love remembers the little visiting nurse who worked her heart out, determined that she was going to cut through the red tape fast enough to see him enrolled at Aux Chandelles before she left the job — and she did!

Love remembers the grandmother who, though she wisely stayed out of the picture once she knew this child was secure in his family, came each year with his Christmas and birthday gifts like a veritable Hannah; wept to see him actually riding the little kiddycar she had brought him . . . rejoiced over every inch of progress she was able to observe from one year to the next.

O My Mother, when I think of all the Hannah-gifts my children would have received at your hands, had you stayed longer! And yet — and yet, somehow you did keep giving them gifts through the years, and now the Inward One writes from those thousands of miles across seas and continents to say it:

"You wrote a line awhile back about your mother's death — true, physically she didn't share much in the life and lives of our family. Somehow, though, she stands out more clearly in my mind than the grandparents whom I knew "in the flesh." Maybe it's a "reality" which I have fabricated, but I think I know Grandmother Sieber through you and through (Aunt) Liz pretty well — and even in life we all conceive personalities quite differently — so who can say that my knowledge of her is not real? Some people live on *through* their children; others maybe live on *with* their children — so that we can know them both quite separately and well. . . ."

Love remembers the one who kneeled to shake hands with BuBu — a stranger. And then this child, in an unprecedented response, solemnly leaned and kissed the cheek of the kneeling man. How is it that the Little Guy sensed what we found out only much later — that the Big Man who looked into his eyes that day was the father of a special child?

Love remembers the perfect responses of love. . . .

"You know," says our Anne, "I could have a child like him. And though I'd hope for a normal child, knowing him has taught me how much fun and satisfaction is possible even when everything doesn't turn out as you'd hoped!"

(Years later, thousands of miles away, this Anne and her husband present us with our first grandchild — a perfect, bonny boy who is called by the Little Feller's name. . . .)

Love remembers the fun of it all. . . .

He is *three:* he is sick, he is miserable. Yet, miserable as he is, he is clever enough to enjoy this illness to the hilt. Two pillows, please.

And *facing* the TV — *on*, of course. A pacifier is demanded. Great-grandmother's shawl with the funny patches of bright wool must cover him. Mamma must pull up a chair beside him and hold his hand for a bit. Now he's all set to be sick. All is demanded with a sweetness that's impossible to resist, and this woman doesn't attempt to resist it, for the chance won't come soon again. A day or two, and he'll be well, so independent that we can't even get him on a lap. . . .

He is *four*, and he has witnessed, these winter evenings, much chess-playing in the living room. He too would like to play, and makes power-grabs for the chessmen, only to find himself very unpopular indeed. But to-night one of the boys heeds the urgent noises and pointings which clearly indicate his challenge to any comer. The chessmen are set up; Little Feller, crawling on all fours, drags up a big chair and seats himself with importance. He begins the game with fervor. Chin on little uncoordinated left hand, he simulates a moment of thought, then, pawn-in-hand, he takes mincing jumps all over the board, removing this queen, that knight, another bishop, in a grand coup, always careful to place *his* winnings on *his* side of the board. Finished with his clever move, he waits obediently for his rival to show his skill. But we all know — as he knows — who will win. . . .

He's *five*, and it's been a long day. But now that Other Significant Person comes through the door, briefcase in hand. Shriek after shriek of pure joy shatters our rooms. *The Micklemouse* is borne aloft; *The Prince* is kissed and carried, taken for a walk, fed, bathed, diapered, treated to a stream of nonsense names which this Abba has always showered on his small children. I smile. I've heard of proper people who not only insist on naming their children names that cannot be nicked, but never call the child by any but his Proper Name. Abba, alas, doesn't know any better! But if he needs justification for his lack of propriety, let it be in the words of the Chinese proverb:

A CHILD THAT IS
LOVED HAS MANY NAMES

The love of our neighbor in all its fullness simply means being able to say to him: "What are you going through?"

Simone Weil

5

"Caring . . .
Is All That Matters"

Hot day in the crowded waiting room at Crippled Children's Clinic. *Waiting* Room. Now there's an example of precise English usage. *Waiting* Room. *Wait* here with that wiry infant who can't walk, can't crawl, can't sit, can't *wait*. Who flails in your arms from 8:30 A.M. until — sometimes — 11:30. *Wait* with the child who crawls now, but can't crawl on *this* floor, in *this* crowd. . . . *Wait* with this eager-beaver who now lurches about in braces, falls flat, laughs to escape your clutches, falls flat, cheerfully gets up, lurches, grabs the nearest leg or dress, makes for the stairs, for the Coke machine, for the waste-bin. . . . *Wait* your turn. . . . *Wait* until the doctors have come, until they are out of "consultation," until the child's name is called. One learns to *wait* in this room.

But your apprenticeship has been thorough. You didn't learn it all here. In between bouts with the Waiting Room you have been schooled at home. The simplest actions which before BuBu were not even time-measured become painful exercises in the art of Waiting.

Peeling potatoes for dinner. Sounds simple, and once it was. Now — ten potatoes, seventeen interruptions. Drop the peeler in the sink; wipe hands on apron; run to save the child, or the stereo, or the window, or the cello, or the few green plants you have dared to keep. Now return (SMILE!) to the half-peeled potato, take up the song where you left it — if it happens to be that good a day — and add a few more strokes of the peeler, a few more measures of the song before you intervene for the thirteenth time.

UP WE GO! You could carry him — you'd like to — and you'd be up in no time at all. Who measures the time it takes to go up the stairs? But he needs to go alone, swaying dangerously from one step to the next, and you are playing the waiting game right behind him. It has to be this way; he must do it alone. But you have to be there. The next step will likely be the one he misses. Somebody has to be there when he misses it. (How do you improve each shining hour in this painful process of going upstairs?)

Now you're at the top. Your patience is stretched taut. It has taken the two of you five minutes to climb the stairs. Every day. Times two, times four.

You think of all the *wait* fragments floating about in that disorderly mind of yours, and somehow they make you furious. . . . "Learn to labor and to wait." That's from grade school days. Stupid Longfellow, you think now, to string those two together as if they were of equal difficulty. . . . "They also serve who only stand and wait. . . ." When did I learn that sonnet? (I was thirteen, mowing Grandma Virtue's lawn, and as I mowed, I checked the words occasionally . . . "On His Blindness" scrawled on lined theme paper and stuck in my belt.) Now even John Milton sounds silly; why is he so defensive about the values of waiting? And David, naive David, to make waiting sound so easy, its rewards so sure, so swift: "Wait on the Lord, be of good courage, and he shall strengthen thy heart."

Wait. Wait for the child to reach the next stair-tread, the next growth-spurt, the next miracle. Wait for the doctors to finish the conference, for the receptionist to finish the red-tape of intake. Wait for the shot to make him drowsy so he won't be terrified to be taken away from you to the O.R. You'd wait gladly, but this time, wouldn't you know it, they tear him away. His brown scared eyes follow you to the last bend of the hall. "Wait here, Mother," the nurse simpers.

His desperate "Ma — ma!" fills the corridor. Why couldn't *they* wait for a change — wait long enough for the medication to work, sparing him this terror?

The Waiting Room at Crippled Children's Clinic, where all the waitings of these years seem to converge — this place has been a sort of River Chebar for you. To sit here among "The Captives" has been, inevitably, to "hear the word of the Lord" as Ezekiel did. For one day you suddenly say: *Waiting shall not have dominion over me.* I shall not be shredded, destroyed by waiting. I'm not going to *fight* it by tensing up over the list of things that aren't getting done because I'm here. . . . I'm not going to *run away from it* by picking up that stale magazine. . . . I'm not going to *sneak around it* by cheating. (Bring the Boy in at ten — say he overslept, the traffic was heavy — anything! . . . *Carry* him upstairs — no one's here to see! . . . Do it *for* him — *once* won't matter!)

No. The way is *through*. And I'll find my way through this waiting ordeal. It's the only way I know to deal with conflict and keep self-respect.

That's when you start being Still. Loose and Light. Free. Free, even in that *Waiting* Room. Free, even with the flailing boy-child pummeling your lap, your shins, your tranquillity.

That's when you begin to see your fellow-captives. See them, hear them, *wait upon them* with something approaching honest attention. You can't, it's true, say, even with your eyes, "I know how you feel, what you are going through. . . ." Because you don't.

In all those six adventures of childbirth you never surfaced to sense that the delivery room was overly cheerful or overly subdued. You never listened to the doctor explain, later, in your private room, about a damaged changeling who was substituted for the perfect baby you had expected. Most of these people here know how that feels. . . .

Your babies — all of them, at one time or another — frightened you by falling from a high chair or a bed. But you never had to carry the guilt of a fall that took away, permanently, the shine from your child's eyes, the brightness from his face.

You never needed to watch your child disintegrating before your eyes from a disease over which there is no control. . . .

Really, thinking back over your life, you've got to admit — haven't you? — that you don't know enough about any suffering to be able to say to another, "I know what you're going through."

There was that childhood of yours, crammed with love and acceptance. A poor family, a fatherless family. But a family in which all were treasured. Treasured by the dead father.

Remember how your mother told you of his death-day? How he kept saying, "Bring the baby in, Bertha" — and she would bring you in and he'd just look at you. She didn't know, but you did, much later, that the repeating of this simple little sentence, "Bring the baby in to me, Bertha" — gave you the incomparable gift of a father's love. . . .

Treasured by the strong mother you were, all of you; and by brothers and sisters who always let you know how they felt about you — with kisses, gifts, words, and sometimes with pinches, scratches, bites, and slaps.

There were the awkward, exhilarating teen-years peopled with loyal friends of your own age-group; smiled upon by adults who believed you were going to do something good with your life, and let you know they believed.

There was, at the end of college and that horrible year of teaching, marriage with a man of integrity who was loving enough to ignore your eccentricities, big enough to welcome your independence. With him you were able to make — not a perfect marriage, but what is better — a *good* marriage.

There were children. Bright. Healthy. Not a flaw. . . . Think of it — all those precarious tree-houses, hut-fires ("Poor Mommy," your little Comforter would say, watching her brothers dragging out yet another tangle of boards for yet another construction, "Are you *very* tired of Huts?") — all those ticky-tacky rafts on Jacob's Creek — and never a broken bone or serious injury of any kind! . . . There were children . . . children who have caused you only the normal amount of anxiety. Children who, it turns out, seem to care much about persons and ideas, little about getting and spending, and who have made a happy mother out of you without destroying your personhood.

In your whole galaxy of relatives you didn't know of a divided or broken home, and few instances of great personal tragedy. You never knew the loss of any of your flesh-and-blood by death — except for the normal, expected — however painful — loss of parents.

This . . . has been your life. So how could you say to anyone, "I know what you are going through"? Except, of course, when the talk turns to general confession: "We have left undone those things which we ought to have done; and we have done those things which we ought not to have done." There you could put in an authentic word or two.

But one day you received a slightly damaged child and by default (you had no choice, really) you found yourself saying *Yes*. So you learned to wait. So you're here today in the hot *Waiting Room*, forty-eight years old, and feeling slightly damaged yourself.

And perhaps you are beginning — just beginning — to understand that though you cannot say, "I know what you are going through," it may yet be possible to learn to ask Simone Weil's question that has haunted you all these years: "What are you going through?"

What are you going through?

The Waiting Room is stifling. Two hours, nearly three, you've waited, all of you. Thank God, BuBu is absorbed, for the moment, in a pull-toy.

And now the first name is called. A spindly boy who has been playing chess with his father nearby pulls himself up and totters to the door, supported by braces and crutches. At the door he signals gaily to the man at your side who is folding up the chessboard. "See ya, Dad!" The father smiles and nods, and the hall swallows up his son. Then he turns to you, reading, somehow, the question in your eyes.

"We had four sons — they all had it — the other three died between their fourteenth and fifteenth year. . . . He's fourteen next week." He looks down at you, smiling brightly as if you have given him some rare gift. (Paralyzed, you've said nothing.) He pats your hand lightly, a comforting gesture.

"It's hard. . . ." He whispers it, still smiling. . . .

Epilogue

Incredible, that I should be sitting here in Capernaum — Kefar-Nahum — Jesus' "own city"! Here all around me are the ruins of a synagogue built, they say, on the foundations of the one standing in Jesus' time. Sparkling Galilee and the heights of Golan are at my back, and I face the *bet-hamidrash* — the teaching court — where Jesus very likely told the stories that have both framed my life and woven themselves into its texture. *The Lost Son, The Lost Sheep, The Unforgiving Servant* — these are Capernaum stories. Here Jairus was a chief ruler when he came to Jesus asking help for his sick child. Here Peter was asked to run down to the docks for the famous fish with the tax money in its mouth.

In the shade of a broken column within the *bet-hamidrash* lies a tiny Jewish boy. His Israeli parents, sight-seers, have left him here in his car-cot for his (and their) comfort. Delighted, I can't help feeling that a very special grace has been given me today — to find here, where Jesus "took a little child and set him in their midst" only one living being, and that a child!

It's good to sit in the heat among the dark basalt ruins and think of another child. Thousands of miles from here he is growing and thriving in the House-on-the-Corner. For somebody *did* come forward. Somebody *did* care enough to disrupt her own life and that of her family, and take over where we left off.

In the year that is passing, the Little Feller has become a Big Boy, developing almost faster than a normal child his age would develop in a given year. He rides his tricycle down the street, I'm told, and can be trusted not to cross to the next street or run out into the traffic. He dresses (more or less) and undresses himself, boards the school bus with aplomb, uses more words and longer sentences daily, and sits through a church service without too much difficulty.

He has put away many of the childishnesses that we, his family, permitted him. We did this partly out of inertia, partly, we admit, out of fear of causing extra strain for a child who was soon to find all the Significant People of his Life leaving him in the hands of strangers.

Will he know us, welcome us when we return in a few months? Will another upheaval cause a regression after the fine progress he has made with Aunt Ruth and her family? I don't lose sleep over such questions. *I believe in Love.*

Shall I be able, after these quiet, easy months on our lovely Judean hillside, to manage a big house, a big household, and a Big Little Boy? Maybe not, but I won't worry. *I believe in the power of Love.*

And shall we be able, this big, crazy family of ours — be able to say *Yes* to this child so completely that no matter what happens to any one of us, his future as a continuing member of that family will be secured? This is another of the waiting questions. Love, I am convinced, will find the answers.

The Author

Author and Son

Miriam S. Lind was born in southern Idaho, where she lived with her mother and five older brothers and sisters. In her early teens the family moved to northern Illinois, where they made a home for her aged grandfather.

Later they moved to northern Indiana where she finished high school, received a BA degree from Goshen College, Goshen, Indiana, and attended a year at the Goshen Biblical Seminary. While living in Goshen, Indiana she was married to Millard Lind and two sons were born here.

Later the family moved to western Pennsylvania, where her husband served as adult curriculum editor for the Mennonite Publishing House in Scottdale, Pennsylvania. During their thirteen years' stay in this location three more sons and a daughter were born. The family then returned to northern Indiana, where her husband is Professor of Old Testament at Associated Biblical Seminaries, Elkhart.

She writes, "I have a strong sense of vocation and conceive of that vocation as 'becoming a human being' — something which seems to require a good bit of understanding and acceptance from family and friends, as well as from myself.

"Not a professional writer (or a professional *anything*) I have, over the years, occasionally turned to writing as an attempt to share 'the grace of life' with other nonprofessionals like myself."

Mrs. Lind is well known as a writer of a regular feature in *Christian Living* for a number of years, for her poetry, and as author of *Such Thoughts of Thee*.